Unpopular Poems

Unpopular Poems

Ronald Duncan

Rupert Hart-Davis LONDON 1969

© Ronald Duncan 1969
First Published 1969

Rupert Hart-Davis Limited
3 Upper James Street
Golden Square, London W1

Printed in Great Britain by
Western Printing Services Ltd
Bristol

SBN 246 98560 7

Contents

Solitudes

No. 1

Love like a storm breaks,
   uproots my serenity.
No limb of me can withstand
   gale of your being.
On the precipice of your eyes,
   I cling to habit,
Clutch at tufts of morality,
   but all's lost, all blown away
By blizzard of your gentleness;
     Seeking to save myself I cry:
     'Oh, love, destroy me utterly.'

No. 2

If they should ask where he found beauty
say: 'in my lips, hair, mouth and eyes,
—easily in my eyes.' Then stare at them
so as to silence them.

No. 3

Confound your jealousy.
What crime have I committed?
Whom have I
   raped, murdered or robbed
That I should now deserve
This punishment of being loved?

No. 4

I had hoped that
    just as coarse grasses and withered weeds
Slowly move in, and in time, completely cover
    a mine tip or a bombed site,
So would habit, work and worry
    eventually camouflage the slagheap of my heart;
And to this end I let any distraction grow:
    labouring to forget you.
Then casually, if not unkindly,
    you visited this wilderness:
And all was ash again.
    Now I have not the strength for any further
Perverse husbandry, and live
    knowing this waste is me.

No. 5

My unhappiness had become a second skin to me:
    Enclosing me completely;
    Something I took for granted: woke to
And lay down in: the part of me I cherished,
Because you were its cause.
    And believing you were happy
I was able to carry my own unhappiness:
    thinking it was a sacrifice to some purpose,
    a condition of your contentment,
Or, at least, a small contribution.

But now that you tell me
That you, too, are unhappy
    I cannot bear the weight of my own any more.
Even so, send all yours to me:
    if he has your laughter,
And I your tears,
    in time, all of you will come back to me.

No. 6

And he reached that point
    When leaves alone listened
And the soil only seemed to understand,
When only the light embraced,
And the night cherished;
When the linnet lay with maggots in its wing.
Now let the thin wind laugh
    over his indecipherable epitaph.

No. 7

If you had died
                    then death
    would have given me
That certainty which is death's certainty;
That mercy which is death's mercy.

But as it is my life's become
   that death you have not died.
I see nothing, looking for you.
I hear nothing, listening to you.
And when I speak, it is because
   I think you are by my side.

No. 8

It rains behind my eyes.
A gale blows through my mind.
The great waves breaking on the beach
Are feeble compared to this tide within me.
Neither women nor work
Can quieten this energy which rages within me.
Only music, only Schubert,
Can contain me; for the rest, it is waste:
That word: my epitaph.

No. 9

I ride, the road winds uphill;
A thin wind blows;
It is raining; it is night.

I ride, the road winds uphill;
A thin wind blows
through my mind;
It rains behind my eyes.
It is night.

I ride a dead horse; the road is lost.
The wind blows through my mind;
It rains behind my eyes;
It is night.

Both the dead horse I ride and the road is lost.
My mind blows;
My eyes rain;
It is night.

My weeping eyes are blown before the wind;
A riderless horse
treads them into the road.
It is night: the night is me.

No. 10

I have now become grateful for my worries,
thankful for my financial difficulties,
and pleased that I have this burden of a farm
with all the repairs of a small estate.

I am obliged to the Inspector of Taxes
who interrupts my meditations;
the telephone's ring is now as much a consolation
as the innumerable forms I have to fill in
with frivolous and irrelevant detail.

Even when I have the toothache, I am glad,
and I give thanks for the nail in my shoe, for anything
That distracts me from the wound, the hurt, the pain of you.

No. 11

There have been many; only one,
   Whose memory does not touch some bruises on my mind.

There have been many; only one,
   whose image is not an accusation:
      regret at the best,
      remorse at the worst,
      either because my kindness was cruel,
      or their cruelty was unkind.
   They loved being loved:
      not fond of me
      but of flattery;
      not faithful to me,
      but to their own vanity.
Your love alone was a gift, not a claim.
   I learn that lesson slowly and
   now let you go again
              with difficulty.

No. 12

Last night I dreamt
That all my fingernails were eyes
And that I strangled Blindness with my hands
till she cried from pain for mercy;
And I showed none,
For I knew that tears alone could give her back her sight.

Then, as she looked, and saw:
   it was as if the sun had vision
   for I threw away my shadows and all the rags of night
   and bathed within the pity,
   for pity is her light.

No. 13

      With silent wings
        I circle round your silence;
      On timeless feet
        I walk towards your absence;
      Behind closed eyes
        I look upon your presence.

No. 14

   In my time, I was here too,
   But you did not notice me sitting there alone,
   Stirring my coffee, smoking interminably
   As though waiting for somebody
     But without an appointment.

   In my time, I knew you too
   But you didn't listen then
   To what I had to say,
   Nor could you find the time
   To read what I had written.
   I remember I once offered you my love.
   In return you gave me a cigarette.

In my time I endured your indifference.
Now I am beyond it: you must keep it to yourself.

No. 15

Loneliness is our thirst.
Other people's loneliness:
    the only water to quench it.

No. 16

Does the wind move the branches
    or the flaying leaves cause the wind?
It does not matter—the wind blows.
Three trees stand there on the bank—two ash, a scrub oak
        between them.
As the gale funnels up the valley
    the two ash trees show pliant, their branches combed by the
        wind:
But the oak stands rigid: then suddenly its great trunk breaks
        asunder.
Which tree is the stronger, the ash that bends
    or the unmoveable oak now too splintered for timber?

No. 17

Lobes of mauve lilac
Lie indolent on the evening air;
Waxed white magnolia, children's hands in prayer;
And over the wall aubretia sprawls
For bees to paddle in its waterfall;
And all about my grazing eyes
A green world in innocence lies.
   Grateful for my solitude I keep
   Company with my thoughts, and fall asleep.

No. 18

Neither health nor happiness
Are as precious as consciousness.
It is better to be conscious of pain or misery
Than unconscious in pleasure.

No. 19

Thou, on a Cross; I, on a divided heart.
No other point of identification, but the nails;
Mine of indecision. Forgive me, for I do know what I do:
   Do to her whom I love, but not exclusively;
   Do to her whom I love, but not completely,
Two hands, two eyes, two legs and two feet:
Choice is not possible, amputation's probable.
Only my love is whole: each is a part of you.

No. 20

Oblivion as a writer,
Death as a man;
This is your future:
   Escape it, if you can.

The Mistress

She possesses me completely;
I am at her mercy: she has no mercy.
One moment, she lies quiet as milk
 the next, she flings the night or my work in my face.
Sometimes, she encourages me and flatters me,
 at others, she scratches till I bleed with remorse,
Her moods are mercurial.
 She is all extremes, entirely inconsistent.
I live alone, only to discover
 Loneliness is just another woman.

Postcard

When all this place is rubble, ash and dross
As it will be, and no-one miss the loss,
When my untidy life has reached its tidy end
And you sit old and cold with memory as a friend,
When the years have worn you,
And worry torn you,
Then read these lines and feel my love again,
Remembering we rode the high places of this world together.

The Gift

Since she whom I love
   has a gift for jealousy;
I–a talent for adultery,
We reached that point where
We kept our friends in conversation;
Lawyers in fees, and ourselves
In something that passed for anger,
But was more like grief.

Now I see I must learn to love
   her jealousy:
   it being a part of her,
And hope that she can love me
   for my adultery.
But this she's done. This she's done.
Could it be her jealousy was a gift,
   A gift to me?
We have begun. It is not done.

For W. S. C.

Our grief is not for his death
   But for our own life which his loss diminishes;
While he lived, he lent us a courage
   We did not possess; a resolution,
To which we were not inclined;
   And by some alchemy made us who were blind
Perceive a vision bright within his mind.

The weary feet, the broken hands, the wounds were ours,
   The fortitude was his. Like a sculptor,
He determined the height that each of us should be;
   Making small men tall, weak men strong;
He carved our history and signed this century with his
     name.

Whatever faults or virtues men have
   This man had them in extremity: being whole in being
Where we exist merely in a part. Sensing this, we, who
     are many
   Mourn for him who, from his own uniqueness,
Made us into that few.
   We grieve for a man we did not meet,
But knew.

The Horse

(written for the Horse of the Year Show)

Where in this wide world can
man find nobility without pride,
friendship without envy or beauty
without vanity? Here, where
grace is laced with muscle, and
strength by gentleness confined.

He serves without servility; he has
fought without enmity. There is
nothing so powerful, nothing less
violent, there is nothing so quick,
nothing more patient.

England's past has been borne on
his back. All our history is his
industry; we are his heirs, he
our inheritance.

Song

In the forest of my dreams
    My fierce desire
Tigers her movements.

By the river that is sleep
    My slow eyes
Serpent her breasts of light.

Like a gorsebush that's on fire
    My quick blood
Stallions her loins of night.

Across the desert of the day
    My blind hands
Weep for her presence.

Song

Now the East Wind
  Hunts the tired year:
Biting with ice,
  Freezing with fear.

By a thorn hedge
  The creature lies;
Even the moor mourns
  As the year dies.

Gently the snow
  Falls on a leaf,
Bending it down
  With secret white grief.

Aria

(*from Christopher Sly*)

When one loves
     It is difficult to sleep;
When one sleeps
     It is dangerous to dream;
When one dreams
     It's a pity when we wake;
For when we wake, the whole world then conspires
To tease our blood and spill our blood's desires.

Aria

(*from Christopher Sly*)

Though other men make love with words
   I can improve upon them.
I court girls with a bouillabaisse
   And tempt them with consomme.
What poets attempt with their praise
   I achieve with roti.
My flattery is in the mayonnaise:
   I seduce them with the souffle.
Though other men make love with words,
   I thus improve upon them.

Plain Song

The revolving Earth
tunes into one of the four seasons
to tease our incompatible desires.
   Spring amplifies our hunger;
   Summer tones down our appetite:
   Autumn records our disappointment;
   and Winter sets us in silence again.

Oh, Earth, busy with fertility,
   wheat and the woman,
   turn and attend to:
   those who are uprooted,
   whose blood wastes into
   warm bathwater apathy–
who with sad frivolity ignore each season,
pursuing comfort for an uncomfortable reason.

Easter Lullaby

Lord Jesus once was a
   child like thee,
    Yet there has been no
    other.
Lord Jesus laughed once
   just like thee,
    For Mary's delight, as
    you delight me.
Weep, child, weep for
   Jesus' Mother.

Lord Jesus once had hair
   like thee.
    His could have been no
    softer;
With skin as smooth and a
   mouth like thee,
    And eyes that had wept
    before they could
    see;
Sleep, child, sleep for Jesus'
   Mother.

Lord Jesus once had toys
   like thee,
    Throw, child, throw your
    ball higher;
And hands that His Mother
   kissed like me,

Hands that my hands
nailed to a tree;
Weep, child, weep for thine
own Mother.

Lullaby

(for Virginia's son)

What falls more lightly
Than lilac to a lawn?
  These eyelids over your tired eyes.

Who grows more gently
Than grass, moss or lichen?
  Your tiny limbs reaching through the loam of night.

What sleeps more softly
Than mole, mouse or kitten?
  Your fragile dreams weaving their unbroken thread.

Who wakes more gaily
Than thrush, lark or linnet?
  I, for the boy of you;
  I, for the joy of you.

The München-Gladbach Lyric

Today, I am sad,
        sad as stone things are
In their stillness;
        or as old toys are
In their loneliness;
        as a room is
That is empty;
        as a child is,
That is lost.

This sadness clothes me
        as sparrows feathers
fit a sparrow's wings;
        closely it lies over me
completely like a panther's skin
        over the panther,
giving its savage stealth
        the quiet sheen of night.
So do I walk, wearing your absence
        like a crimson robe:
Proud of my grief, Prince of our parting.

Let others be beggared in gaiety,
        I will sit here rich in my waiting,
Quiet in my wanting.
        Clothed in this sadness I wear
What you have woven;
        my silence speaks:
All time shall hear
        what this dumb heart has spoken.

Do not Cling to Me Thus

Cantata for St Albans Cathedral   *(for Alan Rideout)*

Chorus of Disciples

And we had gone back to our homes;
But Mary would not leave;
    and stood outside the tomb, weeping.

And when she was alone, she bent down, still weeping,
    and looked inside the tomb,
Where the body of Jesus had lain.

And the next day, we returned and found her there:
    Woman, why do you stay here—
                                still weeping?

Mary Magdalene

Because they have carried my lord away,
And I do not know where they have taken him.

Chorus

And as she said this,
    A man appeared, standing there.
    It was Jesus.
And Mary turned, not knowing she turned to Jesus.

Tenor

Woman, why are you weeping?
For whom are you seeking?

Mary Magdalene

If it is you who has carried the body of my love away,
    for pity's sake tell me where you have put him,

And I will bury his body with my hands
And heal his wounds with my grief.

Chorus
And he turned to her and said:

Tenor
Mary.

Chorus
And she looked up and replied:

Mary Magdalene
Master.

Tenor
Mary, do not cling to me thus
    While I am yet a man.
Mary, do not look at me thus
    While I have not yet gone to my father.
Mary, with your arms about me,
    and your eyes before me,
You hold me here in the world of man.
Mary, if you love me, do not cling to me thus.

Mary Magdalene
Jesu.

Tenor
Mary.

Chorus

And she let him go.
And he rose from her love,
And he rose from his love:
To a love that is greater
Than human love.

Flotsam

Christ, is this Thy Cross, tossed
by a wave at my feet, complete
morticed and set and wet
with a blunt nail through the white deal wood?
Made in a hurry and thrown on to some poor fellow's pillow
lifting and enveloping.
If Thy Cross, Christ, can in spite night's
storm and day's tempest ride tide,
the gale's lust and the sleet, and keep
an unknown appointment so punctually, surely
I should find You more easily, especially
as You lie in my heart like a green leaf in an old book
revealed, if only I could find my heart, open it, and look?

Ascension

It was not that I raised myself to Him
   But that He reached down for me.
And during that time, after they had found the tomb empty,
I was among them.
   Seeing me, Mary Magdalene embraced me.
   'Do not cling to me thus,' I cried
   'While I am still a man.'
   'What a man loves, he does become.'
   For two days, I wept at her grief for me.
   For two days I walked beside her
      sharing no burden, casting no shadow.
   It was not that I had risen from the dead
      but love had not died in me.

Then, as I watched them disperse
back to the nets, the loom, and the last
   from which I'd called them,
I saw their disappointment that the Kingdom I had brought,
had not been the Kingdom they had sought,
The only crown I wore,
Scratched my forehead badly;
The only throne I knew,
Pattered on four little hooves.
And as I watched them and walked with them I wondered
   whether I had not sinned greatly:
      by burdening their innocence with a vision they couldn't
         share;
      by confusing them, setting father against son, son against
         father.

I stood for a moment observing Peter
   dexterously mending the mesh in his net,
And in that moment I saw the whole tapestry of tears
   which I had woven:
Two thousand years, with less love at the end of it;
And I saw Charity's long crusade of savagery;
Tolerance turning to bigotry and faith to the thumbscrew.
And seeing all this and foreseeing all that
With so few, so few, not even twelve to understand,
I walked on, leaving no footprints save in my remorse.
   The earth I loved had hands.
   It held me by the feet.

Then in the garden, that garden, I suffered a second agony;
   their nails, gentle to these nails,
   their cross light to this cross: the realisation
That I should not have projected the struggle within me
   but should have lived it internally:
   denied myself, betrayed myself, judged myself and thus
   given man
   that love he could not give me: a compassion
   beyond the Passion.
That was the thought which crucified me.
Forgive me, for I knew what I had done.

It was not that I raised myself to Him
   but that He, in great mercy, reached down for me.

Canticle

(for Thomas Eastwood)

If gratitude is a prayer
Then even I can pray;

2

Those who have walked
The dark unending corridors
Of their own despair, and have trod
That corkscrew stair where
Regret leads and remorse follows,
and who have known that distress
when the thought of suicide
came as a caress, they who have stepped back from such sadness
they alone know gladness.

3

Now my eyes laugh for their light;
my veins sing for my blood;
My days are all delight
Since I know each hour's been stolen
from that womb where only maggots quicken.

4

Therefore I sing, grateful for the sun
which tigers the blue prairie of the sky
stalking the fallow moon which bleeds with darkness
till the udder of the light
is milked and it is night.

5

And I who have imagined I was laid
Within that damn indifference of the grave,
Must sing of fire: glad for its warmth,
Glad for its friendly flames.

6

And my moist lips must speak
That word which is the most important to them: 'water, water',
With my throat's gratitude I repeat: 'water, water'.
May the fingers of the rain touch me;
May the hands of the river play over me.

7

If my eyes could speak they would sing
praise for the shape of each and anything,
grateful for each colour too,
especially for that gentleness
which clothes the fields with green,
the sky with blue.

8

And if my feet had tongues, they would show
gratitude for the earth they trod on,
the earth that yields us,
waits to receive us.
    Oh Earth, I am in love with thee,
    As with a woman, I am in love with thee.

9

To be is to accept life in its entirety.
I am grateful for pain
which alone can measure
the mercy that is sleep;
I am grateful for sorrow;
Is sorrow not the lawn
on which joy dances?
Yes, even for Death I am glad;
For death gave me
This gratitude for life.
    Oh Life, I am in love with thee,
    As with a woman, I am in love with thee.

Carol

Where the earth floor was puddled with
   urine; damp straw
In the manger; draughts under the door.
But it was appropriate that He
   should be born there
               who was to live in me.

Then the crowds bored and listless,
   a few stop to jeer,
The rest move off to watch a juggler.
But it was right that He
   should speak there
               who tried to speak to me.

Where the rough nails were driven
   with malice, his hands
clutch a poppy and the petals drip.
But it was just that He
   should bleed so,
               who had to bleed for me.

And those two women weeping
   who washed his feet with tears,
Tears for Him and for each other.
But it was as well they
   should cry so
               who had to weep for me.

Impromptu for Briony

Whose blood is this
That bleeds upon the rose?
To whom does
      the quiet grass grow?

Whose tears are these
Now falling from the sky?
Whose grief drags out the tide?
Whose sorrow fills the sea?

Whose hope is it
Which lifts the blackbird's wing?
Whose joy is it
That makes this sweet bird sing?

The joy is His, the grief is His;
His sight looks through your eye;
The hands you use, the feet you wear
Are His, as these words too.

Epitaph on an Unknown Passenger

Having descended the escalator at Queensway Tube Station
and walking towards the platform on my way to Leicester
    Square,
  I heard a man running up behind me,
  as if he were being pursued,
  or was racing to catch the last train:
which was odd, since it was during the morning.
  He caught up with me just as I was turning a corner:
   his coat tails flying,
   his spectacles falling to the ground.
    'Excuse me,' he cried as he passed me, 'excuse me,'
  and he ran on to the platform.
And there I saw him fling himself in front of the train
  as it emerged from the tunnel.
As they dragged his corpse from the line
I wondered what sort of man this was
  who, while chucking his life away,
  had clung on to his good manners.

Saint 'Orace's Lament

(from Saint Spiv)

Let us thank God for the dark:
   without it
Many would have no place to hide.
       Let us thank God for the dark.

Let us praise Him for the Poor:
   without them
The Pools could give no gladness.
       Let us praise Him for Poverty.

Let us bless Him for War:
   without it
Peace would be 'orrible.
       Oh let us bless Him for War.

Let us thank Him for sickness:
   without it
How could we know we were well?
       Let us thank God for boils, ulcers,
         tumours and cancers.

Let us praise Him for death:
   without it
Some of us wouldn't look alive.
       Let us thank God for Death.

Let us thank Him for Drunks;
   without them
I wouldn't know I was so sober.
       Let us praise Him for Aspirins.
       O Allelujah. Sing Alka Seltzer.

To M.

No logical contradiction
    between us;
but merely, a complete
    lack of connection, now.

Written on a girl's table-napkin at Wiesbaden

If he were to walk into this cafe
I doubt if you'd notice him
Nor know how long he sat there alone
Stirring his coffee, perhaps smoking one cigarette after another

As though waiting for somebody
But without an appointment,
Nor would you notice that he was gone.
If he walked beside you, you would quicken your step.
And if he spoke to you with his slow eyes
You would look away and order another cocktail.

You would mistake his gentleness for effeminacy.
You would call his kindness, weakness.
You would have no time for him.
So why not take off that crucifix round your neck
    And hang a corkscrew there?

Ballad of Stratton Gaol

Great souls in prison cells
lie
   and commit no perjury
   but to themselves do injury,
   farming their mind's boundless demesne
   for a harvest of fears, dreams and worry.
To their sorrow, pain comes as a relief,
Pain comes as mercy to the confined saint and common thief.

There's my friend Gandhi
who
   prays and spins, then spins and prays,
   patiently passing endless days,
   a man no Empire could dismay
   nor he an Empire or himself betray,
for under his leathern skin he too holds a prisoner:
his proud spirit which, humbled, is his power.

And then dear Mauberley,
where
   he is I do not know, but fear
   for him, for he knew no fear
   nor unlike many did he disappear
   to Canada with Europe's chaos near.
Where he had made his home, he stayed in loyalty,
spoke out his mind to be accused of treachery.

God, what an age is this
when
   prisons are improvised and filled

before they're built. Those who are killed
get off with half the captive's addled
safety. For one it's blood, the other tears are spilled.
It's all the same to us–'Pro bono patria.'
Let's place all double beds in storage for Utopia!

There was a couple
who
   lived where I was living;
   She waters her garden, biting
   her nails, waiting, looking and waiting
   for the post from the prisoner who's pining
for news of the girl who's waiting–which may sound pathos
but is for all that true, and to their dance sheer damn loss.

Where do I come in?
I am.
   For what? For salving from the sea
   thirty gallons of petrol–for me!
   And using same for purposes of husbandry.
   Poor husbandry! Poor me! Both wedded to poverty!
Now my cows unmilked; some stacks open; some corn
     uncarried.
Here I am by four white-washed walls confined, no little
     worried.

But I am not alone,
a fly
   shares my captivity, and he
   shares my restlessness for home and he,

like my mind, flits endlessly and fruitlessly,
both of us passengers to the same futility.
But between the fly and I is this disparity:
In weight; we share the same fixed gravity.

Stratton Gaol 1943

Lines for N.S's First Birthday

You stand upon the lip of an abyss
Which mankind took a million years to cross.
Yet within twelve months you will leap
Across this same glacier of time
And from your sweet dumb stare you'll reach
easily to the easy miracle of speech.
Then Prince of Words, Emperor of a phrase
          you'll share that throne
Where Donne and Dante sit. As their heir
their language shall be yours
And all poetry, your own.

For a Dying Woman

She lies propped up by pillows,
Her pink hands clutch the sheet like a bird's feet in the snow.
Her eighty years heavy in her eyes,
Shawled loosely round her shoulders.
They say she is frail. I do not see frailty.
What rock is there strataed in darkness
Diamond with strength of will?
Or where is there a river flowing
So that its tide can ebb and flow at its own volition?
Compared to her a gale is listless
And every star is impotent, for every star is dumb.
Life does not lie in mobility,
But only in consciousness.
I do not send her flowers, but this
    her own life that is in her,
the articulated point in a blind and dumb universe.

Envoi

The purpose of life
　　　is to increase awareness, sensitivity.
It follows that the meaning of life
　　　is to suffer, first in oneself,
Then for the other.
　　　The meaning of life is to suffer.